# SPACE FRONTIERS

## Space Technology

**Helen Whittaker**

A⁺

This edition first published in 2011 in the United States of America by Smart Apple Media.

Smart Apple Media
P.O. Box 3263
Mankato, MN, 56002

First published in 2010 by
MACMILLAN EDUCATION AUSTRALIA PTY LTD
15–19 Claremont Street, South Yarra 3141

Visit our website at www.macmillan.com.au or go directly to www.macmillanlibrary.com.au

Associated companies and representatives throughout the world.

Library of Congress Cataloging-in-Publication Data

Whittaker, Helen, 1965-
    Space technology / Helen Whittaker.
        p. cm. — (Space frontiers)
    Includes index.
    ISBN 978-1-59920-575-5 (lib. bdg.)
    1. Astronautics—Juvenile literature.  2. Space flight—Juvenile literature.
    3. Astrophysics—Juvenile literature.  I. Title.
    TL793.W4928 2011
    629.4—dc22

                                    2009038481

Edited by Laura Jeanne Gobal
Text and cover design by Cristina Neri, Canary Graphic Design
Page layout by Cristina Neri, Canary Graphic Design
Photo research by Brendan and Debbie Gallagher
Illustrations by Alan Laver

Manufactured in China by Macmillan Production (Asia) Ltd.
Kwun Tong, Kowloon, Hong Kong
Supplier Code: CP  December 2009

Acknowledgments
The author and the publisher are grateful to the following for permission to reproduce copyright material:

Front cover photos of the *International Space Station* seen from space shuttle *Atlantis*, courtesy of NASA/HSF; Earth from space © suravid/Shutterstock; blue nebula background © sololos/iStockphoto.

Photographs courtesy of:
Digital Vision, 7 (Moon); ESA-S.Corvaja, 2009, 15; ESA-J.Huart, 6 (satellites); Robyn Beck/AFP/Getty Images, 6 (radio telescopes); Scott Barbour/Getty Images, 5;

James A. Sugar/National Geographic/Getty Images, 11; © sololos/iStockphoto, 6–7 (blue nebula); Marc-Andre Besel and Wiphu Rujopakarn, Large Binocular Telescope Observatory, 9 (top); NASA, 7 (space probes, X-ray), 24, 28; NASA/DOE/Fermi LAT Collaboration, 13 (bottom); NASA Glenn Research Center Collection photo by Quentin Schwinn, 23; NASA/GRIN, 17; NASA/Jim Grossmann, 13 (top); NASA/HSF, 3, 6 (rockets); 7 (manned spacecraft, rovers, space stations, spacesuits), 20, 25, 26 (right), 29; NASA/JPL, 22; NASA/JSC, Eugene Cernan, 4; NASA/MSFC, 21, 26 (left); NASA/MSFC/Pat Rowling, 30; NASA and STScI, 7 (space observatories); NGST, 14; NOAO/AURA/NSF, 6 (optical telescopes), back cover; Photodisc, 6 (Earth); Photolibrary/Photo Library Science/SPL, 12 (top); Photos.com, 9 (bottom).

Images used in design and background on each page © prokhorov/iStockphoto, Soubrette/iStockphoto.

# CONTENTS

## Glossary Words

When a word is printed in **bold**, you can look up its meaning in the Glossary on page 31.

# SPACE FRONTIERS

A frontier is an area that is only just starting to be discovered. Humans have now explored almost the entire planet, so there are very few frontiers left on Earth. However, there is another frontier for us to explore and it is bigger than we can possibly imagine—space.

## Where Is Space?

Space begins where Earth's **atmosphere** ends. The atmosphere thins out gradually, so there is no clear boundary marking where space begins. However, most scientists define space as beginning at an altitude of 62 miles (100 km). Space extends to the very edge of the universe. Scientists do not know where the universe ends, so no one knows how big space is.

## Exploring Space

Humans began exploring space just by looking at the night sky. The invention of the telescope in the 1600s and improvements in its design have allowed us to see more of the universe. Since the 1950s, there has been another way to explore space—spaceflight. Through spaceflight, humans have **orbited** Earth, visited the Moon, and sent space probes, or small unmanned spacecraft, to explore our **solar system**.

Spaceflight is one way of exploring the frontier of space. Astronaut Harrison Schmitt collects Moon rocks during the Apollo 17 mission in December 1972.

# SPACE TECHNOLOGY

*Technology is all about using scientific knowledge to solve practical problems. Space technology uses scientific knowledge to solve practical problems related to space.*

## The Special Challenges of Space

Space is a very harsh environment. Materials and machines designed to function in space must be able to survive extremes of temperature and strong **magnetic fields**. They must also be able to endure **radiation** and the impacts of space rocks.

## What Is So Special About Space Technology?

Space technology is often more advanced than technology used in other areas because of the special challenges encountered in space. Some space technologies are adapted by other industries to solve everyday problems.

## What Problems Does Space Technology Aim to Solve?

The practical problems space technology deals with are usually related to one of three areas:
- Observing space
  Example: How can we see farther into space?
- Using space to improve everyday life
  Example: How can we use **satellites** to predict the weather?
- Exploring space
  Example: How can we send people to Mars and return them safely to Earth?

▼ Hybrid and electric vehicles, such as this electric car, use rechargeable lithium batteries, which were originally developed for use in spacecraft.

# MAPPING SPACE TECHNOLOGIES

Some space technologies, such as radio telescopes, never go into space. Others, such as satellites, go no farther than Earth orbit. Only a few space technologies, such as space probes, are designed to venture farther from Earth.

**Optical Telescopes**
see pages 8–9

**Rockets**
see pages 16–17

**Radio Telescopes**
see pages 10–11

**Satellites**
see pages 18–19

## Manned Spacecraft
see pages 24–25

## Rovers
see pages 28–29

## Space Stations
see pages 20–21

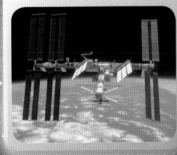

## Spacesuits
see pages 26–27

## Space Probes
see pages 22–23

## Space Observatories
see pages 14–15

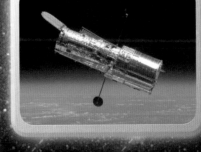

## X-ray and Gamma Ray Telescopes
see pages 12–13

# OPTICAL TELESCOPES

*Optical telescopes collect and focus light from the visible part of the electromagnetic spectrum to make objects in space appear larger and brighter. There are three main types of optical telescopes: refractors, which use lenses, reflectors, which use mirrors, and **catadioptrics**, which use both lenses and mirrors.*

## The First Optical Telescopes

The first optical telescopes, built in the early 1600s, were refractors which had a magnification of just three times, or 3x. Italian astronomer Galileo Galilei improved on the original design by developing a telescope that magnified 33x. Using this telescope, he discovered Jupiter's four largest moons and Saturn's rings.

## How Does an Optical Telescope Work?

The diagram below shows a Newtonian reflector—a type of optical telescope developed by British physicist Isaac Newton in 1669. Light enters from the left and hits the curved primary mirror. The primary mirror focuses the light onto a small, flat, secondary mirror, positioned at an angle of 45 degrees, which then reflects the light into the eyepiece.

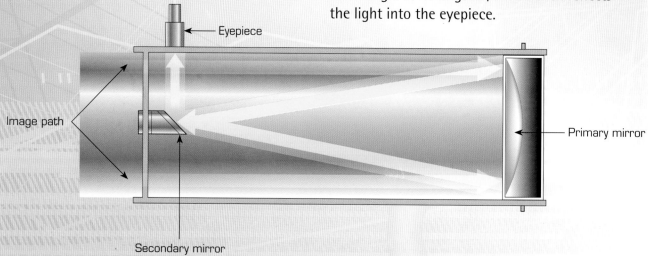

- Eyepiece
- Image path
- Primary mirror
- Secondary mirror

▲ **The Newtonian reflector uses only one curved mirror, which makes it easier and cheaper to produce than more complex designs.**

## Techno-Fact!

Even though the Newtonian reflector was invented more than 300 years ago, variations of the design are still manufactured today and are used by many amateur astronomers.

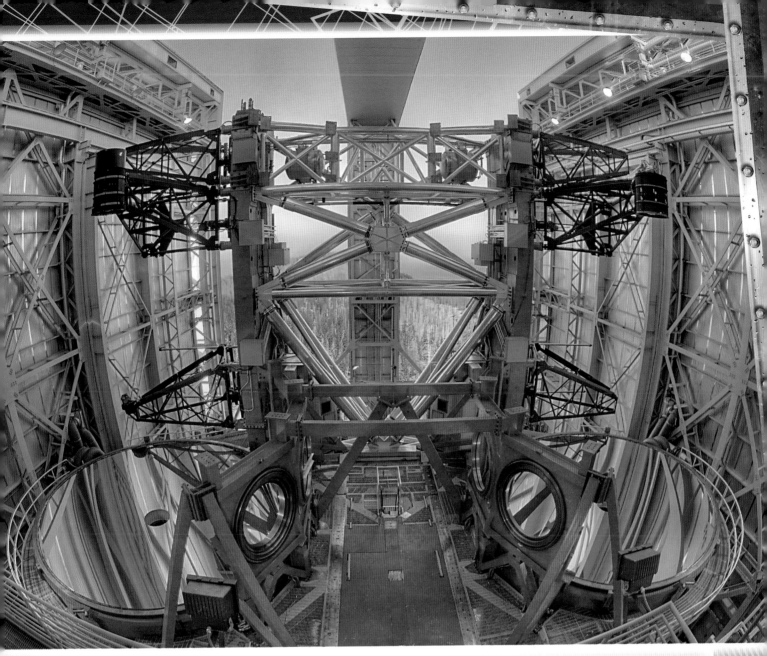

▲ The Large Binocular Telescope in Arizona. It is one of the world's largest optical telescopes. Each of its two mirrors has a diameter of 27.6 ft (8.4 m).

## Optical Telescopes Today

Today, nearly all large optical telescopes used by professional astronomers are reflectors. Reflectors can be built much larger than optical telescopes, because it is easier to build a large mirror accurately than a large lens. Furthermore, the bigger a telescope's mirror, the more light it can collect, which allows astronomers to see fainter objects. Greater size also allows for greater resolution, which means images are clearer.

### Hans Lippershey
#### (1570–1619)

Hans Lippershey was a Dutch–German lensmaker. His "Dutch perspective glass" of 1608 is recognized by many as the first true telescope. A crater on the Moon is named after him.

# RADIO TELESCOPES

*Many objects in space are very faint or cannot be observed at all in visible light but give off radiation at other wavelengths of the **electromagnetic spectrum**. Radio telescopes detect radio waves, which have longer wavelengths than visible light. This means radio telescopes can see things that optical telescopes cannot.*

## How Does a Radio Telescope Work?

A radio telescope has a large, dish-shaped antenna, which receives and transmits radio waves. The dish shape helps direct the collected radio waves to a focal point at the center. Radio telescopes have to be much larger than optical telescopes, because the wavelengths of radio waves are much longer than those of visible light.

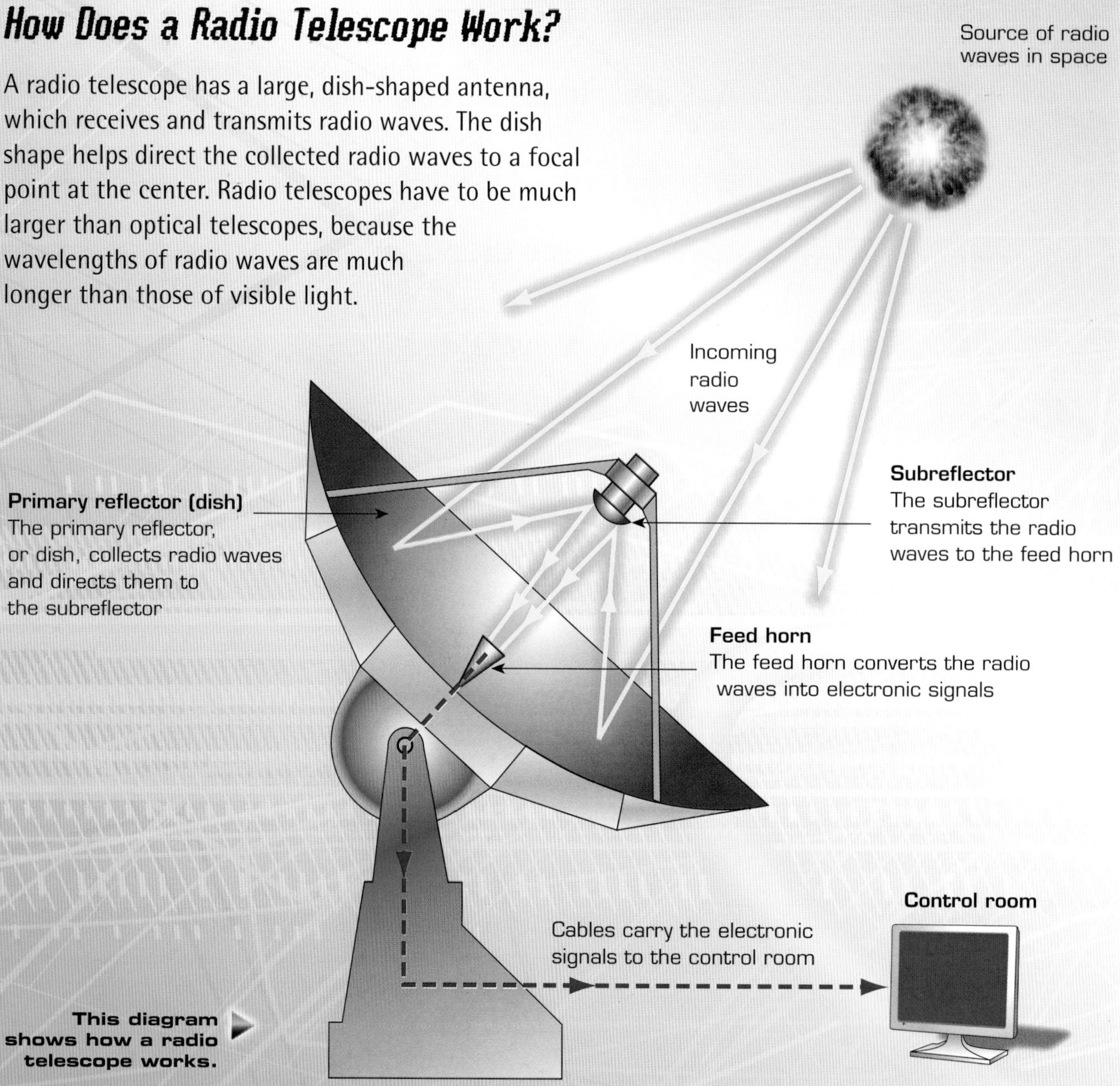

Source of radio waves in space

Incoming radio waves

**Primary reflector (dish)**
The primary reflector, or dish, collects radio waves and directs them to the subreflector

**Subreflector**
The subreflector transmits the radio waves to the feed horn

**Feed horn**
The feed horn converts the radio waves into electronic signals

**Control room**

Cables carry the electronic signals to the control room

▶ **This diagram shows how a radio telescope works.**

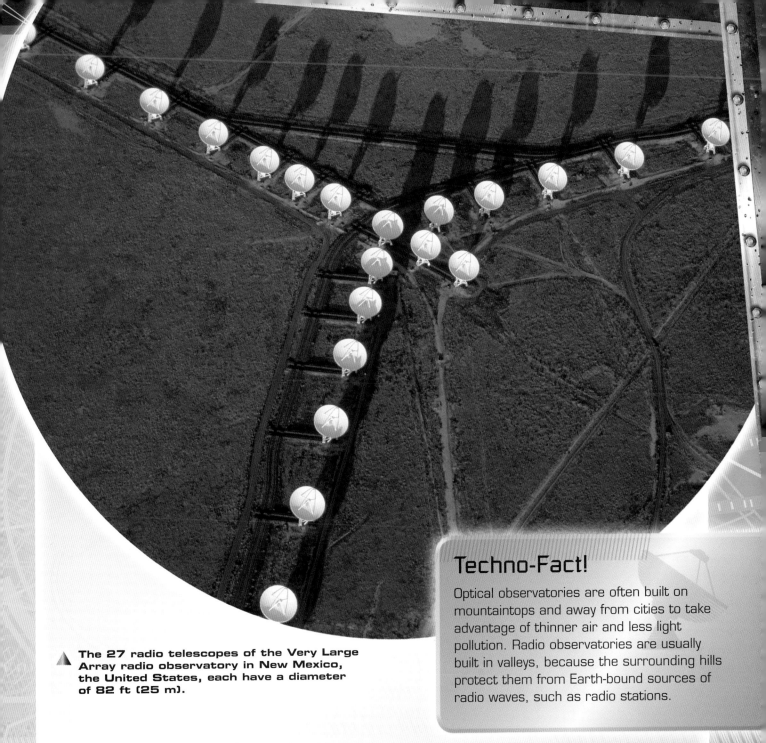

The 27 radio telescopes of the Very Large Array radio observatory in New Mexico, the United States, each have a diameter of 82 ft (25 m).

## Radio Interferometry

When radio telescopes work together, their combined radio waves produce **interference**. The technique of analyzing interference is called radio interferometry. Interference can be used to boost the signal and increase the resolution of images. Radio telescopes which have been arranged to work in this way are called an **array**. The size of the array is the distance between its farthest members.

## Discoveries Made Using Radio Telescopes

Using radio telescopes, scientists have discovered **pulsars**, **radio galaxies**, and **quasars**. It was a radio telescope that helped discover **cosmic background radiation**, too. This provided evidence to support the **big bang theory** of how the universe began.

# X-RAY AND GAMMA RAY TELESCOPES

X-rays and gamma rays are some other wavelengths of the electromagnetic spectrum. They are very energetic and have extremely short wavelengths. X-rays and gamma rays are absorbed by Earth's atmosphere. This means devices which detect them have to be sent into space.

## How Does an X-ray Telescope Work?

X-ray telescopes are attached to high-altitude balloons and satellites. Normal reflectors do not work with X-rays, which are absorbed by the mirror instead of reflected into the eyepiece. X-ray telescopes contain many highly curved mirrors coated with iridium (a hard metal) or gold. The mirrors are placed inside one another and positioned so that the X-rays strike them at a very low, glancing angle.

## Wilhelm Röntgen
### (1845–1923)

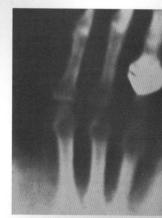

Wilhelm Röntgen was a German physicist. He discovered X-rays in 1895 and, only weeks later, took the first X-ray photograph— of his wife's hand (right). He was honored for his work in 1901 when he became the first person to win the Nobel Prize in Physics.

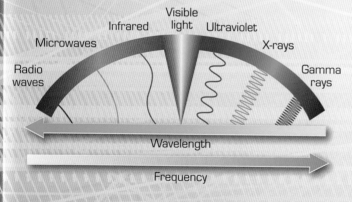

Microwaves · Radio waves · Infrared · Visible light · Ultraviolet · X-rays · Gamma rays

Wavelength

Frequency

▲ This diagram shows the types of radiation that make up the electromagnetic spectrum. X-rays and gamma rays are at one end of the spectrum, with the smallest wavelengths and the highest frequencies.

## How Does a Gamma Ray Telescope Work?

The Large Area Telescope (LAT), which is the main instrument of the *Fermi Gamma-ray Space Telescope*, has four main parts. The Anticoincidence Detector detects unwanted cosmic rays (particles which are not gamma rays). The Precision Tracker determines which direction the gamma rays are coming from, and the Calorimeter measures how much energy they have. The Data Acquisition System then analyzes the information collected by the other three components.

## What Discoveries Have X-ray and Gamma Ray Telescopes Made?

Among the most interesting discoveries made by X-ray and gamma ray telescopes are gamma ray bursts. These are short, random flashes of gamma rays from deep space, whose cause is still unknown. Possible sources of gamma ray bursts include extremely massive stars exploding to become black holes or a pair of neutron stars colliding.

## Techno-Fact!

The *Fermi Gamma-ray Space Telescope* consists of two main instruments. The GLAST Burst Monitor detects gamma ray bursts from a wide section of the sky, while the Large Area Telescope focuses on individual gamma ray sources.

▲ The *Fermi Gamma-ray Space Telescope*, launched in 2008, aims to find out how stars and galaxies were formed in the early universe. Seen here is *Fermi's* Large Area Telescope.

## What Do X-ray and Gamma Ray Telescopes See?

For an object to give off X-rays and gamma rays, it must be extremely energetic. Sources of X-rays and gamma rays include some of the most powerful objects in the universe, such as **black holes**, **supernovae**, and **neutron stars**. Ordinary stars, such as the Sun, also produce X-rays and gamma rays.

▲ The *Fermi Gamma-ray Space Telescope* captured this image of the gamma ray sky. This is what the sky would look like if the human eye could detect radiation 150 million times stronger than visible light.

# SPACE OBSERVATORIES

*A space observatory is a **satellite** housing one or more space instruments. There are more than 30 space observatories in orbit around Earth, detecting wavelengths across the electromagnetic spectrum.*

## Features of Space Observatories

Space observatories vary in design, but they all have similar systems.

- Solar panels and batteries generate and store electricity.
- A navigation system keeps the observatory in the correct orbit.
- Scientific instruments, including a main telescope, collect data.
- Communications antennae send the data back to Earth.
- A computer coordinates everything.

## The Benefits and Disadvantages of Space Observatories

Space observatories produce clearer images than Earth-based telescopes and can detect a wider range of wavelengths. On the other hand, space observatories cost more to build and maintain. They also cannot be as heavy or as large as Earth-based telescopes, because they have to fit inside a launch vehicle to be carried into space.

▼ **This labelled illustration of the *Chandra X-ray Observatory* shows some of its many instruments.**

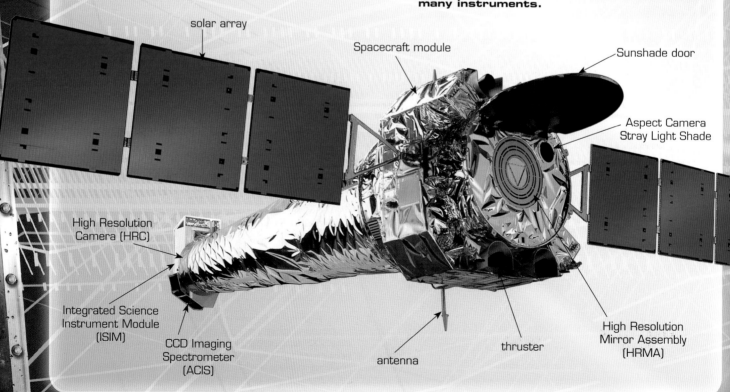

solar array

Spacecraft module

Sunshade door

Aspect Camera Stray Light Shade

High Resolution Camera (HRC)

Integrated Science Instrument Module (ISIM)

CCD Imaging Spectrometer (ACIS)

antenna

thruster

High Resolution Mirror Assembly (HRMA)

## Techno-Fact!

The *Herschel Space Observatory's* primary mirror is 11.5 ft (3.5 m) in diameter. It was built by joining 12 sheets of silicon carbide together, which were then ground and polished to the correct shape and coated with a layer of aluminum. It is the largest telescope mirror in space.

The *Herschel Space Observatory*, launched in 2009, detects infrared radiation. ▶

## Famous Space Observatories

The table below provides information on some well-known space observatories.

| Observatory | Launch Date | Wavelengths Detected | Facts |
|---|---|---|---|
| *Hubble Space Telescope* | 1990 | visible light<br>ultraviolet<br>near-infrared | *Hubble* detected the first organic molecules on a planet outside our solar system. Organic molecules may be a sign of life.<br>It also found that most galaxies probably have black holes at their centers. |
| *Chandra X-ray Observatory* | 1999 | X-rays | If human eyes were as powerful as *Chandra*, we would be able to read a newspaper from 2,625 ft (800 m) away.<br>If the surface of Earth were as smooth as *Chandra's* mirrors, Mount Everest would be less than 6.6 ft (2 m) tall! |
| *XMM-Newton* | 1999 | X-rays | • *XMM-Newton* has an eccentric (long and thin) orbit, taking it to almost one-third of the distance to the Moon.<br>• It has three X-ray telescopes, each containing 58 mirrors. |
| *Fermi Gamma-ray Space Telescope* | 2008 | gamma rays | • *Fermi* is the most sensitive gamma ray observatory ever launched.<br>The telescope was originally called GLAST (Gamma-ray Large Area Space Telescope). It was renamed *Fermi* after its launch, in honor of the Italian physicist Enrico Fermi. |
| *Herschel Space Observatory* | 2009 | infrared | • *Herschel's* instruments detect faint infrared emissions from very cold objects.<br>Liquid helium is used to keep *Herschel's* instruments cool. The helium is kept at -456.7 °F (-271.5 °C). |

# ROCKETS

In order to use space to improve everyday life, we need to be able to get into space. Rocket technology lets us do this. A rocket is any vehicle that gets its power from a rocket engine. A rocket engine works by releasing mass at high pressure in one direction, which provides thrust in the opposite direction.

## Different Rocket Engines

Most rocket engines get their energy from a chemical reaction. The chemicals used are called propellants. These consist of two chemicals, a fuel and an oxidizer, which helps the fuel burn better. In some rockets, the propellants are solid. These are known as solid rockets. Other types of rockets are called liquid rockets because their propellants are liquid.

## Rocket Engines in Spacecraft

The main rockets in spacecraft are usually liquid rockets. The advantage of liquid rocket engines is that they can be turned off and restarted. On the other hand, liquid rocket engines malfunction more often, because they are more complex. Liquid propellants can also leak and cause explosions. Solid rocket engines are often used as boosters, which provide extra thrust at liftoff.

▼ When a solid rocket engine is ignited, its core heats up and the propellant around it starts to burn from the inside out. This sends exhaust out of the nozzle and creates thrust. Once ignited, the engine cannot be switched off.

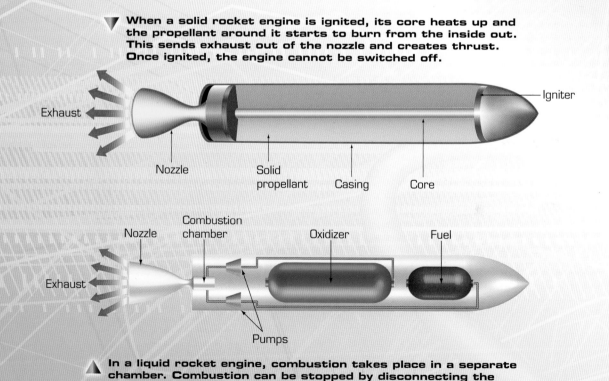

Exhaust

Igniter

Nozzle    Solid propellant    Casing    Core

Nozzle    Combustion chamber    Oxidizer    Fuel

Exhaust

Pumps

▲ In a liquid rocket engine, combustion takes place in a separate chamber. Combustion can be stopped by disconnecting the pumps between the propellants and the combustion chamber.

## Famous Space Rockets

One of the best-known rockets is the United States's Saturn V, which took the first men to the Moon. The **Soviet Union**'s Soyuz range of rockets was first launched in 1966 and is still used today, particularly as a supply ship for the *International Space Station*. Europe's Ariane 5 rocket is used mainly for commercial purposes, such as launching communications satellites.

◄ **Robert Goddard invented the first liquid-fuelled rocket in 1926. It was propelled by a mixture of liquid oxygen and gasoline.**

## Timeline: The Rocket

| **1200s** | **1903** | **1926** | **1942** | **1957** | **1961** |
|-----------|----------|----------|----------|----------|----------|
| The Chinese use gunpowder-powered rockets for weaponry and fireworks. | Russian mathematics teacher Konstantin Tsiolkovsky suggests how rockets might be used to reach outer space. | American Robert Goddard builds the first liquid-fueled rocket. | A German V-2 rocket becomes the first man-made object to reach space. | A Soviet R-7 rocket launches *Sputnik 1*, the first artificial satellite. | A Vostok-K rocket launches the first human into space, Soviet astronaut Yuri Gagarin. |

# SATELLITES

Satellites are natural or artificial objects, which orbit another body in space. Natural satellites include the Moon, which orbits Earth, and Phobos and Deimos, which orbit Mars. Artificial satellites are man-made objects, which orbit Earth. The first artificial satellite, Sputnik 1, was launched in 1957.

## Different Types of Satellites

The table below lists some common types of satellites and what each type is used for.

| Type of Satellite | Purpose |
| --- | --- |
| communications | relays television, radio, telephone, and Internet signals |
| astronomical | observes space |
| Earth observation | predicts the weather, collects environmental data, creates maps |
| navigational | provides data for global navigation systems |
| military | destroys enemy missiles and spies on targets |

▶ **This diagram shows the Earth orbits used by different satellites. Any object above geosynchronous orbit is said to be in high Earth orbit.**

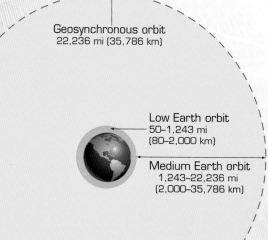

Geosynchronous orbit
22,236 mi (35,786 km)

Low Earth orbit
50–1,243 mi
(80–2,000 km)

Medium Earth orbit
1,243–22,236 mi
(2,000–35,786 km)

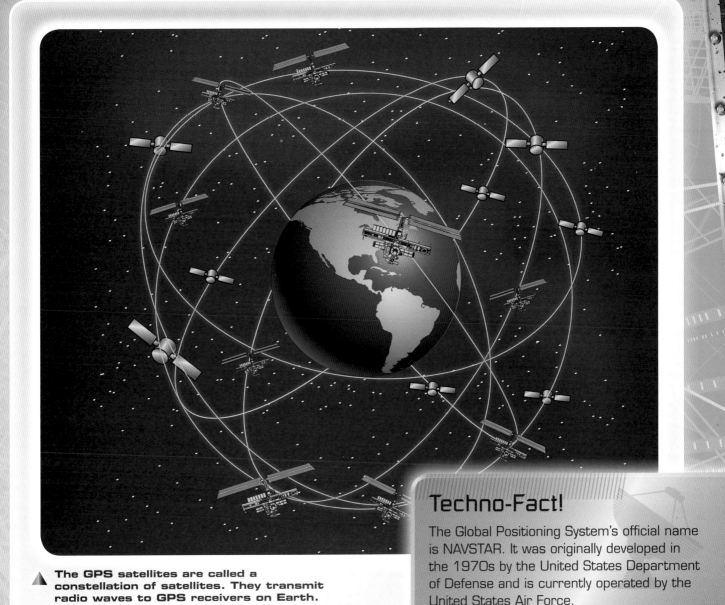

▲ The GPS satellites are called a constellation of satellites. They transmit radio waves to GPS receivers on Earth.

## Communications Satellites

Communications satellites relay signals to and from ground stations. Most of these satellites follow a geosynchronous orbit, which means they orbit Earth in the same direction and at the same speed as Earth's rotation. It also means they are always positioned roughly above the same place on the ground. This makes it easier for ground stations to track them.

## Navigational Satellites

There is only one satellite navigation system currently in operation and it is called the Global Positioning System, or GPS. It uses between 24 and 32 satellites, each transmitting signals to receivers on Earth. The receivers determine the position of the satellites and the distance between the receivers and the satellites. By comparing signals from several satellites, a receiver can calculate its own position very accurately. GPS satellites are in medium Earth orbit.

# SPACE STATIONS

*Space stations are designed to allow humans to live in space. Space station crews conduct scientific research that can only be performed in* **microgravity**, *such as studying the long-term effects of spaceflight on the human body.*

## *The* International Space Station

The only space station currently occupied is the *International Space Station* (*ISS*). The *ISS* is made up of 15 separate modules. These include laboratories as well as **docking** ports, **airlocks**, and living quarters. When complete, the *ISS* will be 361 feet (110 m) long and will weigh almost 925,200 pounds (419,600 kg). It is due to be completed in 2011, but the *ISS* is already the largest space station ever constructed.

### Techno-Fact!

Robotic arms, which were developed to help build the *International Space Station*, have been adapted for a range of uses on Earth, from performing surgeries to dealing with hazardous materials.

▼ **This photograph of the *International Space Station* in June 2008 was taken by a crew member on board the space shuttle *Discovery*.**

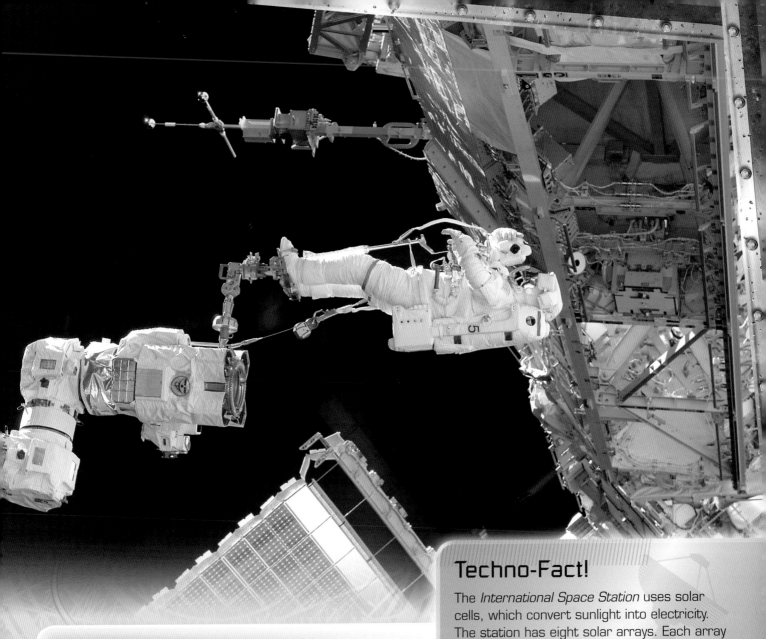

American astronaut Rick Mastracchio works on the *International Space Station* in August 2007 while anchored to the space shuttle *Endeavour's* robotic arm.

## Techno-Fact!

The *International Space Station* uses solar cells, which convert sunlight into electricity. The station has eight solar arrays. Each array is 114.8 ft (35 m) long and 39.4 ft (12 m) wide and has about 33,000 solar cells.

## Building the ISS

Over the course of more than 40 missions, space-walking astronauts constructed the *ISS*, using tools similar to those used on regular construction sites, such as cranes, hand tools, and power tools. In space, however, tools must be tied to something to stop them from floating away. Performing construction work in a spacesuit and in microgravity takes a lot of training.

## Life-support Systems on the ISS

The life-support system on the *ISS* controls the quality of the air the astronauts breathe and the water they drink. It also maintains a comfortable air temperature, Earth-like air pressure, and deals with waste products. One waste product is carbon dioxide, which the astronauts breathe out. A buildup of carbon dioxide in the air would be lethal.

# SPACE PROBES

Space probes are unmanned spacecraft designed to explore planets, moons, and other bodies in space. Some simply fly past their target. Others spend months or years orbiting it. Some have even landed on their target's surface.

## Space Probe Systems

Space probes vary widely in design, but most of them have a number of systems in common.

**Techno-Fact!**

The space probe *Voyager 1* is traveling toward the outer reaches of the solar system and is currently the farthest space probe from Earth.

| Systems Found in a Space Probe | What It Does |
|---|---|
| attitude and guidance | controls the spacecraft's position and speed, and the direction in which it is pointing |
| command and data handling | acts as the spacecraft's "brain" |
| communications | relays data to and from Earth |
| power | generates, stores, and distributes electricity |
| propulsion | consists of the spacecraft's engines |
| scientific instrumentation | collects scientific data |
| thermal control | controls the spacecraft's temperature |

The National Aeronautics and Space Administration's (NASA) *Dawn* space probe is placed inside a thermal vacuum chamber, where it is tested to make sure it will work in the harsh environment of space.

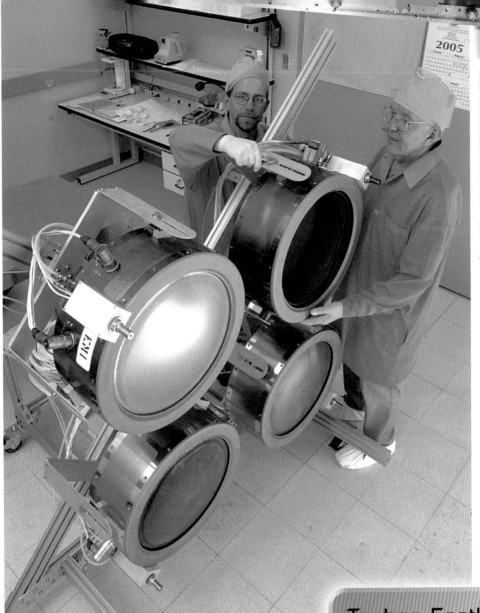

## Techno-Fact!

Technology that was originally developed to make images taken by space probes clearer is now used in medical scanners to produce detailed images of the inside of a patient's body.

## Propulsion

A space probe relies on a separate launch vehicle to get into space. The space probe's onboard propulsion system is used to control its path once in space and to enter orbit or land when it reaches its target.

Some modern space probes use an advanced type of electric engine called an **ion** thruster. This engine creates thrust by accelerating ions of xenon gas. Compared to a rocket engine, it creates a very small amount of thrust, but it consumes propellants very slowly, making it ideal for long journeys.

## Power

Without electrical power, none of a space probe's systems would work. Most space probes that operate in the inner solar system use solar panels to generate electricity. Those that travel to the outer solar system, where the Sun's energy is weak, usually have electrical generators powered by **radioactive** materials, such as plutonium.

# Manned Spacecraft

Manned spacecraft have to cope with the same challenges as space probes, but their design is even more complex, because they need to be bigger and they must also support life.

## Early Manned Spacecraft

The Soviet Union's *Vostok 1* was the first manned mission to space. The spacecraft consisted of a spherical descent, or **reentry**, module and a cone-shaped instrument module, which housed the engines. The United States's *Mercury* spacecraft was a tiny, cone-shaped capsule with engines at the front and rear. Both spacecraft were very cramped and carried just one person.

## Techno-Fact!

The *Vostok* astronaut had to eject from the spacecraft during descent and land by parachute. The *Mercury* astronaut stayed inside the spacecraft, which parachuted into the sea.

▼ This illustration was used by NASA to show visitors the layout of the small and snug *Mercury* spacecraft in 1959. The capsule was only 6.6 ft (2 m) long and 6.2 ft (1.9 m) in diameter.

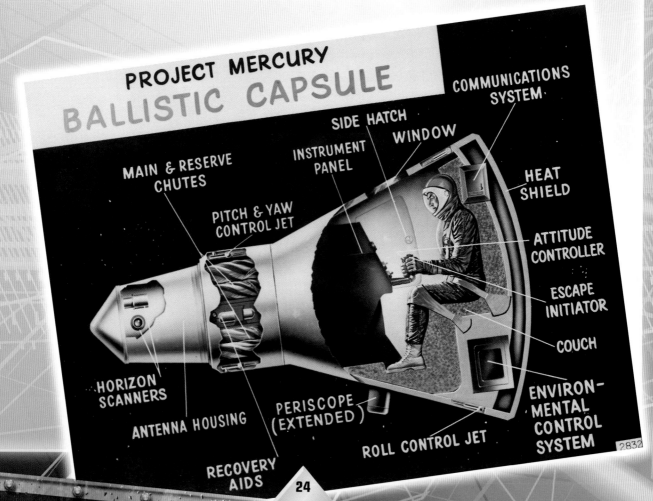

PROJECT MERCURY BALLISTIC CAPSULE

COMMUNICATIONS SYSTEM

SIDE HATCH

WINDOW

INSTRUMENT PANEL

HEAT SHIELD

MAIN & RESERVE CHUTES

PITCH & YAW CONTROL JET

ATTITUDE CONTROLLER

ESCAPE INITIATOR

COUCH

HORIZON SCANNERS

ANTENNA HOUSING

PERISCOPE (EXTENDED)

ROLL CONTROL JET

ENVIRON-MENTAL CONTROL SYSTEM

RECOVERY AIDS

2832

# Modern Manned Spacecraft

Russia's Soyuz spacecraft was first launched in 1966 and is still in use today. The design of China's Shenzhou spacecraft is based on the Soyuz but is much bigger. The United States's Space Transportation System, or space shuttle, was revolutionary in design. It was the world's first reusable spacecraft. Its vehicle is a winged **orbiter**, which glides back to Earth.

## Comparing Modern Manned Spacecraft

Manned spacecraft have changed significantly since the days of Vostok and Mercury. They are much bigger and can carry more astronauts into space, as shown in the table below.

|  | Soyuz | Shenzhou | Space Transportation System (space shuttle) |
|---|---|---|---|
| Height | 24.54 ft (7.48 m) | 30.34 ft (9.25 m) | 184.1 ft (56.1 m) |
| Diameter | 8.92 ft (2.72 m) | 9.19 ft (2.8 m) | 28.5 ft (8.7 m) |
| Approximate weight | 15,917 lb (7,220 kg) | 17,284 lb (7,840 kg) | 4.5 million lb (2 million kg) |
| Number of crew | 3 | 3 | 7 |

# SPACESUITS

*Spacesuits enable astronauts to work outside a spacecraft. Astronauts also wear special pressure suits during a launch and reentry to increase their chances of surviving an accident.*

## Why Do Astronauts Need Spacesuits?

A spacesuit acts like a mini-spacecraft for one person. It protects an astronaut from the vacuum of space, extremes of temperature, radiation, bright sunlight, and tiny, bullet-like particles of dust or rock. It provides the astronaut with air to breathe and water to drink. Without a spacesuit, a human being would die after only a few minutes of exposure to the hostile environment of space.

▼ The first spacesuits, such as this one, were based on the pressure suits worn by high-altitude aircraft pilots.

▲ Modern spacesuits, such as this EMU (extravehicular mobility unit), look very different from the first spacesuits.

## Techno-Fact!

The protective suits that firefighters wear are made out of fire-resistant fabric that was first developed for use in spacesuits.

Technology for Exploring Space

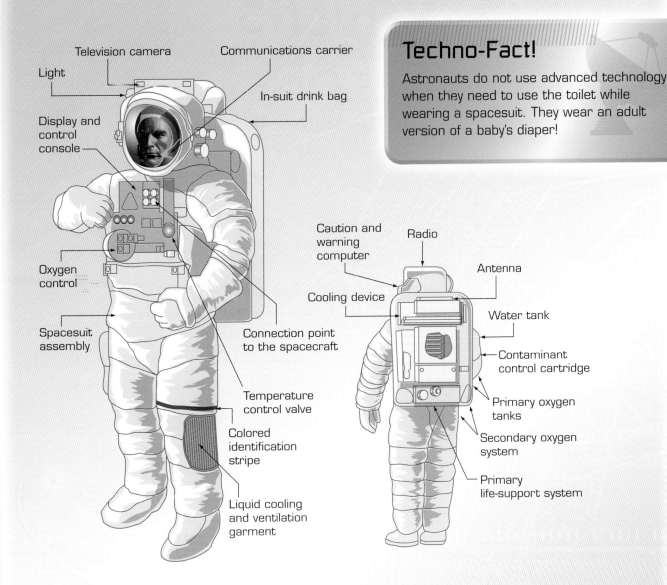

Light

Television camera

Communications carrier

In-suit drink bag

Display and control console

Oxygen control

Spacesuit assembly

Connection point to the spacecraft

Temperature control valve

Colored identification stripe

Liquid cooling and ventilation garment

Caution and warning computer

Radio

Antenna

Cooling device

Water tank

Contaminant control cartridge

Primary oxygen tanks

Secondary oxygen system

Primary life-support system

▲ **The EMU is the spacesuit used by NASA's astronauts when working outside a spacecraft.**

## Parts of a Spacesuit

The spacesuit's underwear has tubes woven into it. Water is pumped through the tubes, keeping the astronaut cool. The main suit is made up of several parts, including an upper body section, which is often hard, sleeves, gloves, pants, boots, and helmet. A backpack houses the life-support system. The astronaut controls everything from a control console on the front of the suit.

## Layers in a Spacesuit

The inner layer of the main suit keeps air in so that the spacesuit stays pressurized. The next layer is strong, nonflexible, and holds the first layer in place. This is followed by five layers of aluminum-coated **Mylar**, which act as a heat shield. The extremely tough outer layer contains Teflon (used in nonstick coatings) and Kevlar (used in bulletproof vests).

# ROVERS

A rover is a vehicle designed to move around on the surface of a planet or moon. So far, rovers have visited just the Moon and Mars.

## Types of Rovers

Most rovers are unmanned. Rovers on the Moon can be controlled from Earth, but Mars rovers are usually independent of human control. This is because Mars is so distant that radio signals take about 20 minutes to make the round trip. A manned rover is driven by an astronaut. It needs to be larger and stronger than an unmanned rover in order to accommodate the astronaut.

▼ This labelled illustration shows the different systems of the Mars Exploration Rovers. The twin rovers, *Spirit* and *Opportunity*, began their exploration of Mars in January 2004.

Navcam

Pancam

Low Gain Antenna

High Gain Antenna

Solar arrays

Instrument Deployment Device

In-situ Instruments

## Timeline: The Rover

**← 1970**
The Soviet Union's *Lunokhod 1* lands on the Moon and becomes the first successful rover landing.

**1971–1972**
The United States's Lunar Roving Vehicle is brought to the Moon by the *Apollo 15, 16,* and *17* spacecraft.

**1973**
*Lunokhod 2*, the second Soviet lunar rover, lands on the Moon.

**1997**
The United States's *Mars Pathfinder* releases the *Sojourner* rover on Mars.

**2004–present**
The United States sends the Mars Exploration Rovers, *Spirit* and *Opportunity*, to opposite sides of Mars.

**2012 →**
*Curiosity*, an American rover, is due to land on the red planet.

This photograph shows the *Apollo 17* lunar rover on the Moon. A new lunar rover was taken to the Moon on each of the final three Apollo missions. The rovers are still there.

## Techno-Fact!

NASA is developing a new lunar rover. It is more like a truck than a buggy, with 12 wheels and a pressurized cabin. It will allow a crew of two astronauts to travel long distances in comfort, without wearing spacesuits.

## Lunar Roving Vehicle

The Apollo Program's lunar rover had to be large enough to carry two astronauts, all their gear, and many rock samples. It also had to be small and light enough to fit on the tiny **lunar module**. To solve this problem, the rover was made of aluminum, a strong but light metal. It also had a central metal hinge so it could be folded in two.

## Curiosity

*Curiosity* is an unmanned rover that relies heavily on new technology. To land on Mars, it will be lowered from the main spacecraft on a cable. The rover has been designed to roll over obstacles up to 29.5 inches (75 cm) high, and it will analyze the Martian soil, rocks, and atmosphere in greater detail than any previous rover. It is scheduled to launch in 2011 and will arrive on Mars in 2012.

# THE FUTURE OF SPACE TECHNOLOGY

What technologies will be developed in the future to help people observe space, use space to improve everyday life, and explore space? Some technologies are already in development, and others may be developed farther into the future.

## Coming Soon

In 2007, 14 space agencies from around the world released "The Global Exploration Strategy," a document that outlined their plans to work together to develop new space technologies. These plans include developing the technology needed to establish a permanent base on the Moon and to send the first humans to Mars.

## Techno-Fact!

NASA's Constellation Program, which aims to send astronauts back to the Moon by 2020, involves a lot of new technology. Scientists and engineers are designing two new launch vehicles, a new crew vehicle, a new lunar **lander**, a new rover, and even new spacesuits.

## Looking Farther Ahead

In the next few decades, scientists and engineers will design a spacecraft capable of flying to Mars. Farther into the future, they may devise methods of launching spacecraft without using rockets. In the very distant future, spacecraft crossing **interstellar space** could become reality.

As shown in this artist's impression, a "space elevator" could one day transport spacecraft. An electromagnetic cable would extend from the surface of Earth to a transfer station in geosynchronous orbit. Space vehicles would use this cable to make their way into space.

# GLOSSARY

**airlocks**
chambers in a spacecraft that allow astronauts to move in and out of the spacecraft without affecting its air pressure

**array**
an arrangement of similar objects

**atmosphere**
the layer of gases surrounding a planet, moon, or star

**big bang theory**
the theory that the universe expanded from an extremely dense and hot state and continues to expand today

**black holes**
regions of space where gravity is so powerful that nothing can escape, not even light

**catadioptrics**
type of optical telescope that uses a combination of mirrors and lenses

**cosmic background radiation**
a form of electromagnetic radiation that fills the universe but is not associated with any space object

**docking**
the process of joining one spacecraft to another

**electromagnetic spectrum**
the range of all possible wavelengths of electromagnetic radiation, including radio waves, microwaves, infrared, visible light, ultraviolet, X-rays, and gamma rays

**interference**
patterns produced when two or more electromagnetic waves interact with each other

**interstellar space**
the region of space starting at the edge of the solar system and extending to the edge of the Milky Way

**ion**
an atom or molecule that has an unequal number of protons and electrons, giving it a positive or negative electrical charge

**lander**
a spacecraft designed to land on a planet or moon

**lunar module**
a vehicle that is part of a spacecraft and designed to land astronauts on the Moon

**magnetic fields**
regions of forces generated by electric currents

**microgravity**
weightlessness, a phenomenon experienced when orbiting a planet

**Mylar**
a thin, light, reflective film made from a type of plastic

**neutron stars**
very hot, small, and dense stars, left behind by supernovae

**orbited**
followed a curved path around a more massive object while held in place by gravity; the path taken by the orbiting object is its orbit

**orbiter**
a spacecraft designed to orbit a planet or natural satellite

**pulsars**
rotating neutron stars that emit a beam of electromagnetic radiation, which can only be seen when the beam is pointing towards Earth

**quasars**
the highly energetic cores of active galaxies, believed to be powered by supermassive black holes

**radiation**
energy emitted in the form of waves, such as those found in the electromagnetic spectrum, which may be harmful to living things

**radioactive**
having or producing harmful energy caused by the breaking up of atoms

**radio galaxies**
galaxies that emit a lot of radio waves

**reentry**
the process of reentering Earth's atmosphere after a spaceflight

**satellites**
natural or artificial objects in orbit around another body

**solar system**
the Sun and everything in orbit around it, including the planets

**Soviet Union**
a nation that existed from 1922 to 1991, made up of Russia and 14 neighboring states

**supernovae**
exploding stars

# INDEX